CHESTER'S

PIANO DUETS

VOLUME ONE
Written and Arranged by Carol Barratt

This book is dedicated to all my pupils, especially Rachel, Linda, Harriet, James, Joanna, Louisa and Anthony

Dear Teacher,

These duets are intended for use in conjunction with the Chester Easiest Piano Course Book 2. In addition, by following each five-finger position indicated at the top of every page, they can be used by any beginner.

First and Second Player parts are of equal difficulty so that the pupil may become familiar with the entire piece.

The fun and invaluable experience of ensemble playing should be encouraged from the earliest days, and these duets are designed to develop a strong sense of rhythm, phrasing and dynamic shading.

Enjoy the music!

Carol Barratt

This book © Copyright 1980, 1991, 1995 Chester Music.

Illustrations by Sarah Lenton
© 1995 Sarah Lenton.

Unauthorised reproduction of any part of this publication by
any means including photocopying is an infringement of copyright.

Chester Music Limited
(A division of Music Sales Limited)
14/15 Berners Street, London W1T 3LJ.

2

AU CLAIR DE LA LUNE

Second Player

French Folk Tune

AU CLAIR DE LA LUNE

First Player

Play this page an octave higher than it is written.

French Folk Tune

TWICE AS NICE

Second Player

Carol Barratt

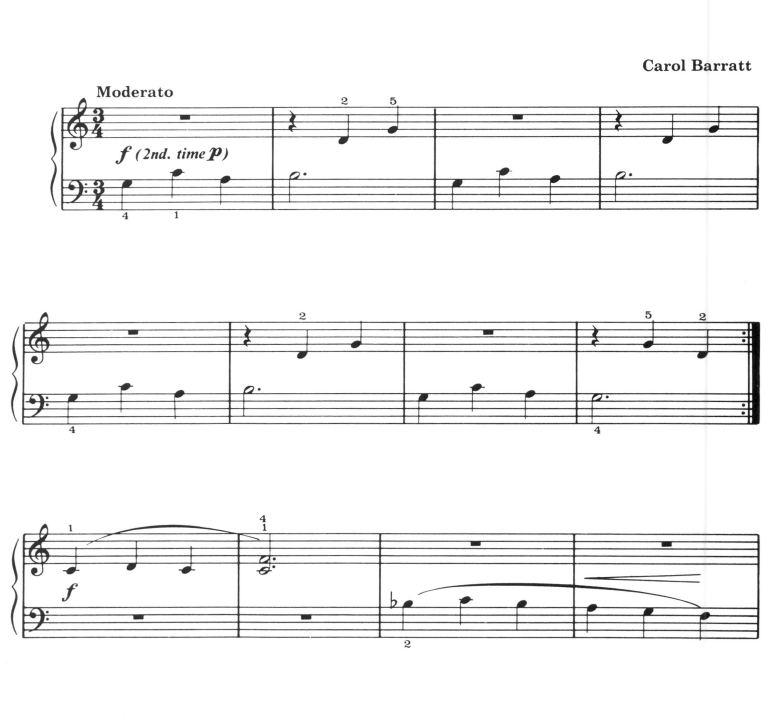

TWICE AS NICE

First Player

Play this page an octave higher than it is written.

Carol Barratt

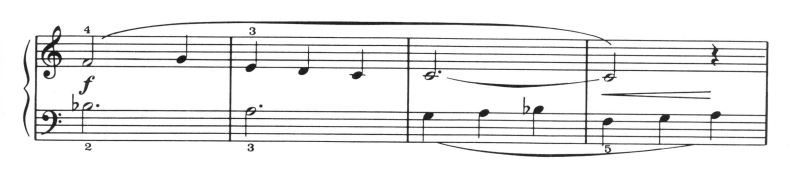

WINTER SONG
Second Player

From D. G. Turk
(1756-1813)

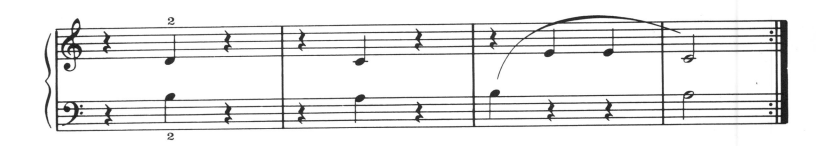

SPRING SONG
Second Player

Watch out for the *p*'s and *f*'s.

From D. G. Turk

Play this page an octave higher than it is written.

WINTER SONG
First Player

From D. G. Turk
(1756-1813)

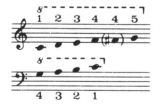

SPRING SONG
First Player

Watch out for the *p*'s and *f*'s.

From D. G. Turk

8

LONDON'S BURNING
Second Player

Play this page an octave lower than it is written.

English Folk Song

LONDON'S BURNING
First Player

Play this page an octave higher than it is written.

English Folk Song

BERCEUSE
Second Player

Carol Barratt

BERCEUSE
First Player
Play this page an octave higher than it is written.

Carol Barratt

ÉCOSSAISE
Second Player

From F. Schubert
(1797-1828)

Moderato

ÉCOSSAISE
First Player
Play this page an octave higher than it is written.

From F. Schubert
(1797-1828)

FESTIVAL DANCE
Second Player

Norwegian Folk Song

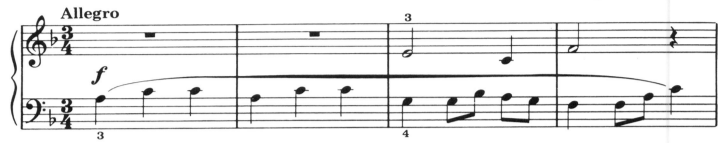

Watch out. The tune is in the Left Hand.

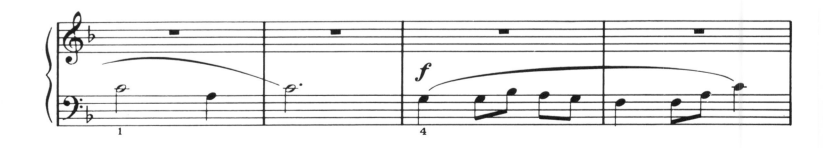

LONDON'S BURNING

Second Player

Play this page an octave lower than it is written.

English Folk Song

LONDON'S BURNING

First Player

Play this page an octave higher than it is written.

English Folk Song

LONDON'S BURNING

First Player

Play this page an octave higher than it is written.

English Folk Song

AU CLAIR DE LA LUNE

First Player

Play this page an octave higher than it is written.

French Folk Tune

FESTIVAL DANCE
First Player
Play this page *two* octaves higher than it is written.

Norwegian Folk Song

GAVOTTE

Second Player

From J. Hook
(1746-1827)

GAVOTTE

First Player

Play this page an octave higher than it is written.

From J. Hook
(1746-1827)

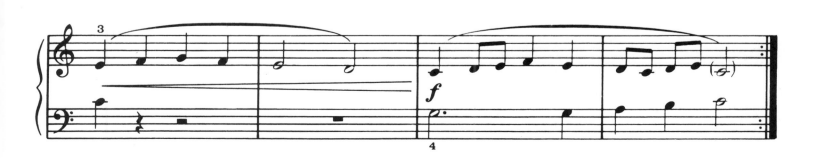

MICHAEL FINNIGAN
Second Player

English Folk Song

MICHAEL FINNIGAN
First Player
Play this page an octave higher than it is written.

English Folk Song

THE LAKE
Second Player

From F. Beyer
(1805-1863)

THE LAKE
First Player
Play this page an octave higher than it is written.

From F. Beyer
(1805-1863)

Watch out . The tune is in the Left Hand.

MOPSTICK RAG

Second Player

Watch out. Both hands are in the 𝄢

Carol Barratt

MOPSTICK RAG

First Player

Play this page an octave higher than it is written.

Carol Barratt

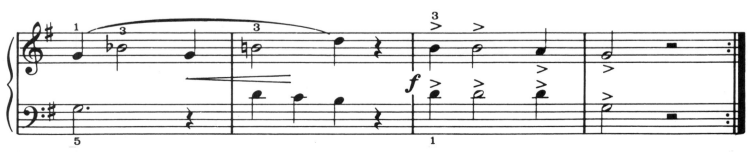

Printed and bound in Great Britain by
Caligraving Limited Thetford Norfolk

04/14(190169)